EYEWITNESS
SHARK

Shark-tooth glove, Kiribati, western Pacific Ocean

Pair of copepods, which stick onto sharks' fins

Undulate ray

Angel shark

Model of a male great white shark

Pair of baby dogfish

EYEWITNESS
SHARK

Written by
MIRANDA MACQUITTY

Shark-tooth
weapon from
the Hawaiian
Islands in
the Pacific

Fossil
tooth of a
Megalodon

Epaulette shark

Shark-shaped gold weight,
from Ghana, West Africa

Shark-tooth
necklace from
New Zealand

Swell shark

DK

Port Jackson shark

Pair of starry smooth-hounds

Fossil of *Ptychodus* tooth

LONDON, NEW YORK, MELBOURNE, MUNICH, AND DELHI

Project editor Marion Dent
Art editor Jill Plank
Senior editor Helen Parker
Senior art editor Julia Harris
Production Louise Barratt
Picture research Suzanne Williams
Special photography Frank Greenaway, Dave King
Editorial consultant Dr Geoffrey Waller
Model makers Graham High, Jeremy Hunt
Special thanks Sea Life Centres (UK)

RELAUNCH EDITION (DK UK)
Editor Ashwin Khurana
Managing editor Gareth Jones
Managing art editor Philip Letsu
Publisher Andrew Macintyre
Producer, pre-production Lucy Sims
Senior producer Charlotte Cade
Jacket editor Maud Whatley
Jacket designer Laura Brim
Jacket design development manager Sophia MTT
Publishing director Jonathan Metcalf
Associate publishing director Liz Wheeler
Art director Phil Ormerod

RELAUNCH EDITION (DK INDIA)
Senior editor Neha Gupta
Senior art editor Ranjita Bhattacharji
Senior DTP designer Harish Aggarwal
DTP designer Pawan Kumar
Managing editor Alka Thakur Hazarika
Managing art editor Romi Chakraborty
CTS manager Balwant Singh
Jacket editorial manager Saloni Singh
Jacket designers Suhita Dharamjit, Dhirendra Singh

This Eyewitness ® Guide has been conceived by
Dorling Kindersley Limited and Editions Gallimard

First published in Great Britain in 1992.
This relaunch edition published in 2014
by Dorling Kindersley Limited, 80 Strand, London WC2R ORL

Colour reproduction by Alta Image Ltd, London, UK
Printed and bound by South China Printing Co Ltd, China

Discover more at
www.dk.com

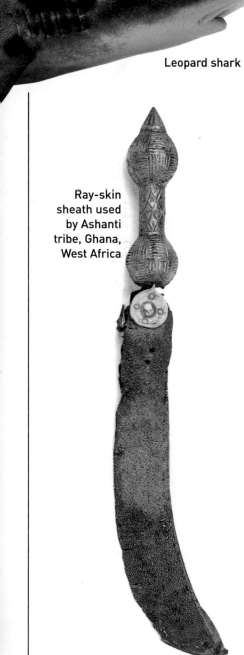

Leopard shark

Ray-skin sheath used by Ashanti tribe, Ghana, West Africa

Long spear for catching sharks, Nicobar Islands, India

Shark rattle, Samoa, South Pacific

Contents

Model of a great white shark

What is a shark?

All sharks are cartilaginous fish, which means that they have skeletons made of gristle-like cartilage rather than bone. These skilful predators range from the dwarf lantern shark at about 20 cm (8 in) long to the whale shark, which can grow up to 12 m (40 ft).

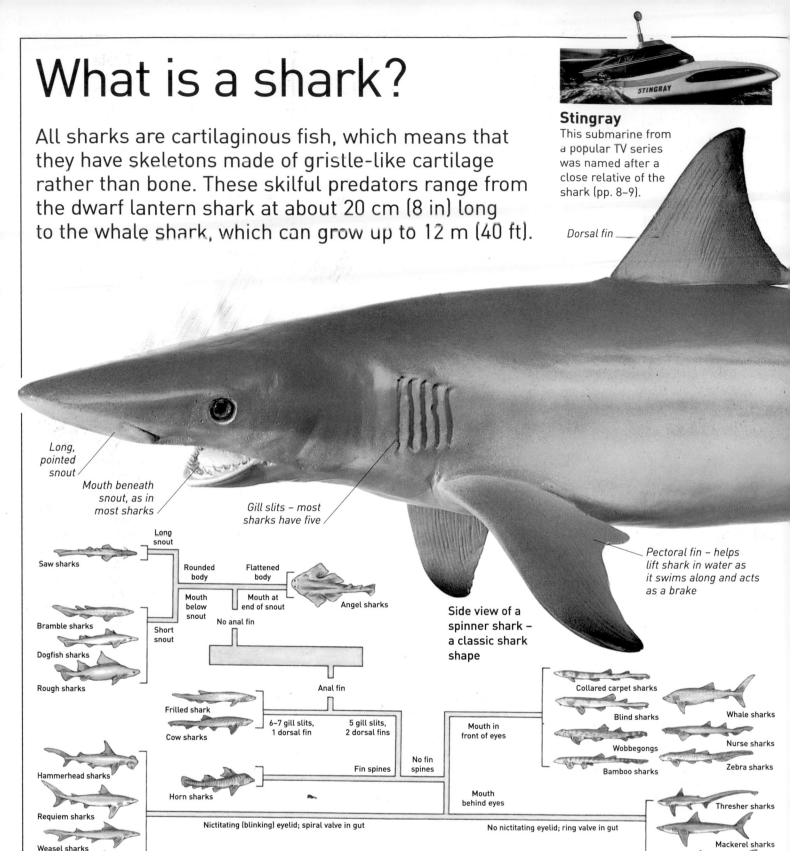

Stingray
This submarine from a popular TV series was named after a close relative of the shark (pp. 8–9).

Dorsal fin

Long, pointed snout

Mouth beneath snout, as in most sharks

Gill slits – most sharks have five

Pectoral fin – helps lift shark in water as it swims along and acts as a brake

Side view of a spinner shark – a classic shark shape

Saw sharks

Long snout

Rounded body

Flattened body

Mouth below snout

Mouth at end of snout

Angel sharks

Bramble sharks

Short snout

No anal fin

Dogfish sharks

Rough sharks

Anal fin

Frilled shark

Cow sharks

6–7 gill slits, 1 dorsal fin

5 gill slits, 2 dorsal fins

Mouth in front of eyes

Collared carpet sharks

Blind sharks

Whale sharks

Wobbegongs

Nurse sharks

Bamboo sharks

Zebra sharks

Hammerhead sharks

Fin spines

No fin spines

Horn sharks

Mouth behind eyes

Requiem sharks

Thresher sharks

Weasel sharks

Mackerel sharks

Smooth-hounds

Basking sharks

Nictitating (blinking) eyelid; spiral valve in gut

No nictitating eyelid; ring valve in gut

Barbeled hound shark

Megamouth sharks

Classification of living sharks

False cat shark

Crocodile sharks

Finback cat sharks

There are more than 450 species of shark. The different species are placed in eight groups, or orders, based on particular body features. When classifying any group of animals, scientists try to work out which creatures are more closely related to each other and put those in a group together. Classification may change when new sharks are discovered or when new relationships are revealed.

Goblin sharks

Cat sharks

Sand tigers

Thousands of teeth

During its lifetime, a shark will replace thousands of teeth. When the front ones wear out or break during feeding, they are replaced by larger, new ones growing in the row behind. Some sharks shed one or two teeth at a time, while others, like spiny dogfish and cookiecutters (p. 45), replace a whole row at a time.

Jaws of sand tiger shark

Skin of bramble shark

Fish scale

Scales

Most bony fish have scales covering their skins. The scales increase in size as the fish grows.

Rough skin

Sharks are covered in tooth-like scales called denticles, which give the skin a rough texture. Bramble sharks (above) have large, thorn-like denticles scattered over their skin rather than covering the whole body.

Shark or fish?

Shark skeletons are light and rubbery, while those of bony fish, such as the bib (below left), are more rigid. Unlike sharks, bony fish have scales instead of denticles and a gill cover, or operculum, instead of gill slits. Bony fish also have a gas-filled swim bladder, which helps to control buoyancy (keep the shark afloat).

Pelvic fin prevents shark from rolling

Anal fin

Tail, or caudal, fin

Spinning around

When hunting in a school of fish, the spinner shark (above) spins in circles to confuse its prey. These sharks grow to 2.5 m (8 ft) long and live in the warm waters of the Atlantic, Indian, and Pacific oceans.

Second dorsal fin

Third dorsal fin

First dorsal fin

Side view of a bib

Barbel (feeler)

Tail fin with same-size upper and lower lobes

Second anal fin

Operculum, or covering for gills

Pelvic fin

Pectoral fin

First anal fin

Air bladder

Ratfish

Chimeras, or ratfish, are distant relatives of sharks and have rat-like tails and beak-like teeth.

Swim bladder of a fish

Full of air

Bony fish have a swim, or air, bladder inside their bodies to prevent them from sinking. Sharks do not have swim bladders and most will sink if they stop swimming. Instead they have oil-rich livers that reduce their weight in water and help to control buoyancy.

Small hook is similar to ones found on fossil sharks (p. 13)

Chimera

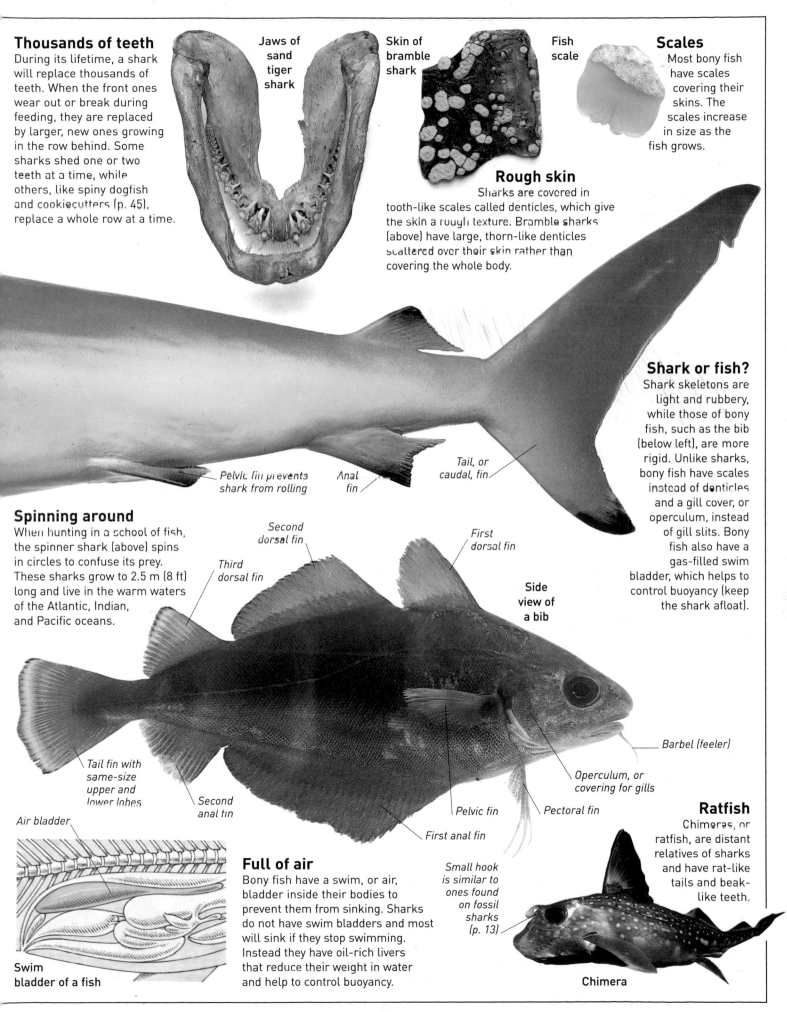

Close relatives

A graceful manta ray swimming with slow beats of its huge wings looks nothing like a sleek reef shark. Yet rays and their cousins – skates, guitarfish, and sawfish – all belong to the same group as sharks. Most rays live on the sea bed where they feed on shellfish, worms, and fish.

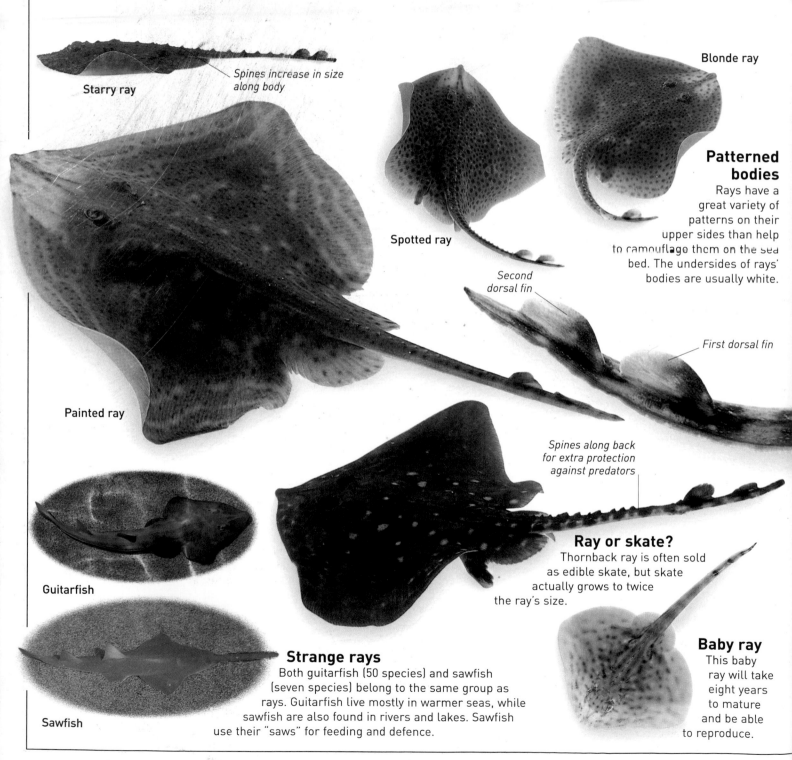

The mighty manta
Manta rays measure up to 7 m (23 ft) across. This female manta, caught off the New Jersey coast, USA, weighed more than 1,300 kg (2,860 lb).

Starry ray

Spines increase in size along body

Blonde ray

Spotted ray

Patterned bodies
Rays have a great variety of patterns on their upper sides than help to camouflage them on the sea bed. The undersides of rays' bodies are usually white.

Second dorsal fin

First dorsal fin

Painted ray

Spines along back for extra protection against predators

Guitarfish

Ray or skate?
Thornback ray is often sold as edible skate, but skate actually grows to twice the ray's size.

Sawfish

Strange rays
Both guitarfish (50 species) and sawfish (seven species) belong to the same group as rays. Guitarfish live mostly in warmer seas, while sawfish are also found in rivers and lakes. Sawfish use their "saws" for feeding and defence.

Baby ray
This baby ray will take eight years to mature and be able to reproduce.

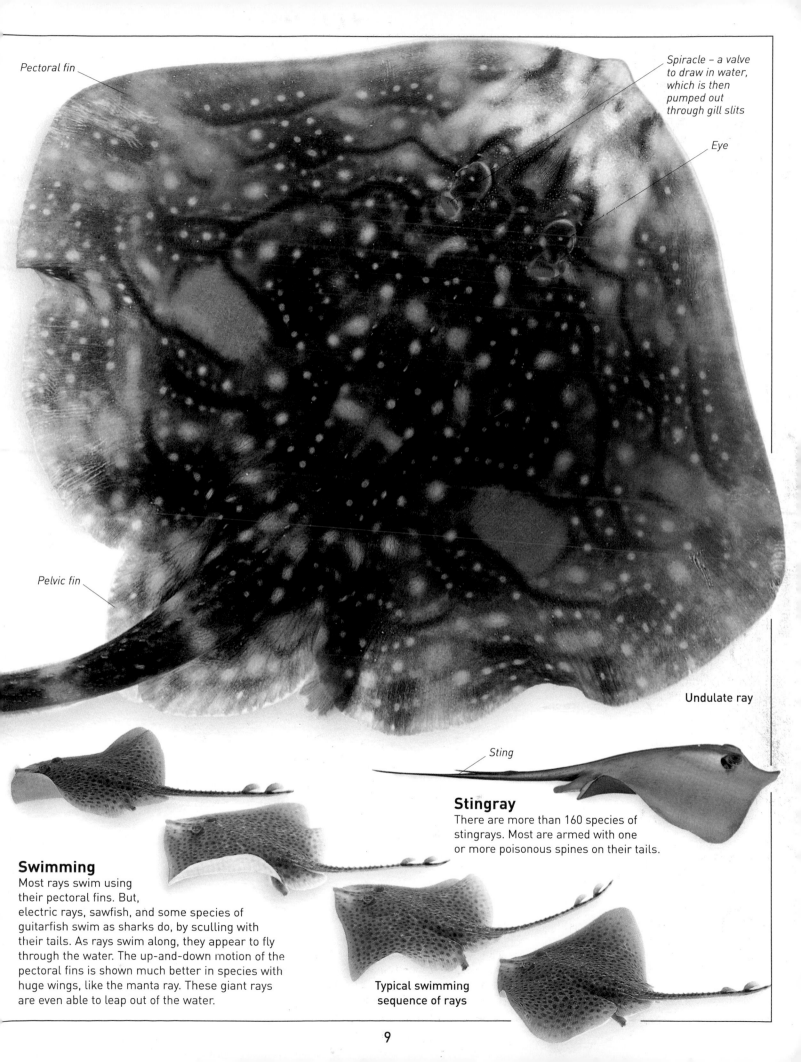

Pectoral fin

Spiracle – a valve to draw in water, which is then pumped out through gill slits

Eye

Pelvic fin

Undulate ray

Sting

Swimming

Most rays swim using their pectoral fins. But, electric rays, sawfish, and some species of guitarfish swim as sharks do, by sculling with their tails. As rays swim along, they appear to fly through the water. The up-and-down motion of the pectoral fins is shown much better in species with huge wings, like the manta ray. These giant rays are even able to leap out of the water.

Stingray

There are more than 160 species of stingrays. Most are armed with one or more poisonous spines on their tails.

Typical swimming sequence of rays

Inside a shark

Packaged inside this spinner shark's body are all the organs that keep it alive. Its gills help it to breathe by taking in oxygen from the water and releasing carbon dioxide back into it. The heart pumps the blood around the body, while the stomach, liver, kidneys, and intestine all play a vital role in the digestive process. Large muscles in the body wall keep the shark swimming, while the skeleton and skin provide support. The brain controls the shark's actions, sending signals along the spinal cord. Finally, sharks, like all animals, cannot live forever and must reproduce to carry on the species. Female sharks produce eggs that develop into baby sharks, called pups. Some sharks lay their eggs in the water, while others give birth to live young (pp. 20–23).

Danger
Sharks have been known to attack people coming down into water.

Paired kidneys regulate waste products

Swimming muscles contract, sending a wave motion from head to tail

Model of a female spinner shark

Vent between claspers for disposing of body wastes

Clasper

Male shark

Female shark (claspers absent)

Cloaca

Claspers
All male sharks have a pair of claspers that are used in reproduction. Female sharks have an opening called a cloaca, through which body wastes are expelled.

Rectal gland (third kidney) passes excess salt out of the body through the vent

Scroll valve in intestine – other sharks have spiral valves

Left lobe of liver

Caudal fin

All in the tail
Sharks have a backbone, or vertebral column, which extends into the upper lobe of their tail, or caudal fin. This type of caudal fin is called a heterocercal tail. The tail is strengthened by flexible rods of cartilage.

Vertebral column

Cartilaginous rod

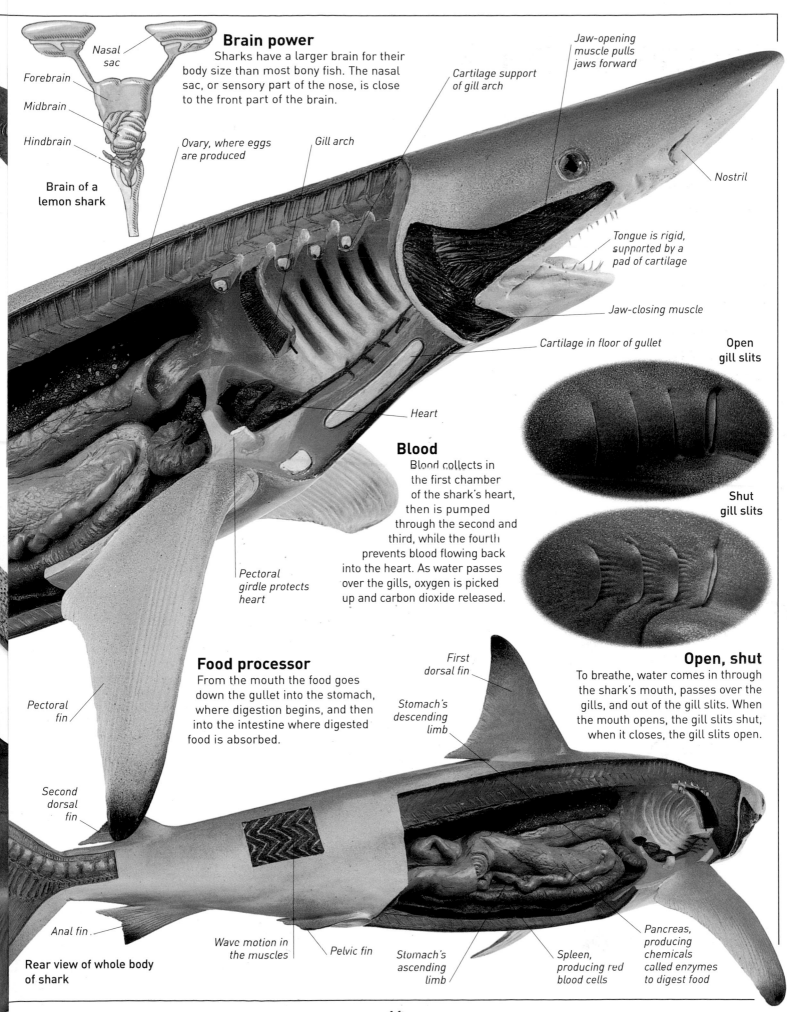

Brain power

Sharks have a larger brain for their body size than most bony fish. The nasal sac, or sensory part of the nose, is close to the front part of the brain.

Nasal sac

Forebrain

Midbrain

Hindbrain

Brain of a lemon shark

Ovary, where eggs are produced

Gill arch

Cartilage support of gill arch

Jaw-opening muscle pulls jaws forward

Nostril

Tongue is rigid, supported by a pad of cartilage

Jaw-closing muscle

Cartilage in floor of gullet

Heart

Pectoral girdle protects heart

Open gill slits

Shut gill slits

Blood

Blood collects in the first chamber of the shark's heart, then is pumped through the second and third, while the fourth prevents blood flowing back into the heart. As water passes over the gills, oxygen is picked up and carbon dioxide released.

Food processor

From the mouth the food goes down the gullet into the stomach, where digestion begins, and then into the intestine where digested food is absorbed.

First dorsal fin

Stomach's descending limb

Pectoral fin

Second dorsal fin

Open, shut

To breathe, water comes in through the shark's mouth, passes over the gills, and out of the gill slits. When the mouth opens, the gill slits shut, when it closes, the gill slits open.

Anal fin

Wave motion in the muscles

Pelvic fin

Stomach's ascending limb

Spleen, producing red blood cells

Pancreas, producing chemicals called enzymes to digest food

Rear view of whole body of shark

Amazing grace

Sharks are graceful swimmers propelling themselves through the water by beating their tails from side to side. Sharks use their pectoral fins to provide lift and change direction. By making changes to the angle of the fins, the shark can control whether it goes up, down, left, or right. Some sharks that live on the sea bed, such as horn sharks (pp. 40–41) and epaulette sharks, can use their pectoral fins to crawl along the bottom. Unlike bony fish, sharks cannot move their pectoral fins like paddles so are unable to swim backwards or hover in the water.

"S" shape
Sharks swim in a series of "S"-shaped curves.

Tail end
"S"-shaped waves pass down the shark's body, pushing it forward (above). The tail bends more than the rest of the body.

Denticles
The denticles on a shark's skin (p. 7) line up with the direction of travel, helping to reduce water resistance.

Cruising
The starry smooth-hound (right) uses its pectoral fins to stay level in the water. The two dorsal fins prevent the shark from rolling.

One-year-old
leopard shark,
38 cm (15 in) long

See how it bends
Leopard sharks have flexible
bodies, so they can turn around
in small spaces. They spend much of
their time cruising close to the sea bed.

Streamlined body
The large pectoral fins of the starry smooth-hound (left) are
held straight out from the body to provide lift and keep the
shark from sinking. When tilted, they can also act as brakes.
The front edge of the fin is rounded and the rear edge is thin, so
that water flows over them more easily. The pointed snout and
tapered body are streamlined to help the shark swim faster.

Full steam
A great white shark
(above) normally
swims at about 3 kph
(1.8 mph). When
closing in on a kill,
the shark puts on a
burst of speed of up
to 25 kph (15 mph).

On the turn
Great whites are not
nearly as flexible as
smaller sharks. They
have to surprise their
prey to catch it.

Tails and more tails

The shape of a shark's tail depends on its lifestyle. Many sharks have tail fins where the upper lobe is larger than the lower. As the tail swings, this lobe produces lift that tends to push the shark's head down. To stop the shark from sinking, further lift is provided by the pectoral fins. In fast sharks, like the mako, the two lobes are almost equal in size. Slow bottom-dwellers, like the nurse shark, have less powerful tails and their swimming motion is more eel-like.

Bonnethead's tail

The upper lobe of a bonnethead's tail is usually larger than the lower lobe. The lobe is held at an angle so it is raised above the shark's midline (an imaginary line drawn from the tip of the shark's snout to the end of its body).

Tail of a bonnethead shark

Tail of a thresher shark

Thresher's tail

The upper lobe of a thresher's tail (left) is as long as its body. The tails of thresher sharks (p. 59) are the longest of any shark and are used to stun prey.

Keel helps the shark to turn

Tail view of a model of a great white shark (pp. 28–31)

Great white's tail

The upper and lower lobes of a great white's tail fin are almost equal in size. The keel on either side of the tail fin helps the big shark to turn.

Angel shark
To lift its huge body off the sea bed, the angel shark beats its tail back and forth while tipping its large pectoral and pelvic fins for maximum lift.

Mid-air mako
Makos are probably the fastest sharks in the sea, reaching speeds of up to 32 kph (20 mph). When caught on an angler's line, they leap clear of the surface in an effort to escape (above). The mako's tail is the same shape as that of the tuna, another fast swimmer.

Lower lobe of angel shark's tail fin (pp. 36–37) is longer than upper lobe

Nurse shark's tail
Slow-moving nurse sharks use their tails (right) for cruising along the sea bed.

Swell shark's tail
Swell sharks spend the day resting on the sea bed. Their tails (right) are held just above their midlines.

Horn shark's tail
The horn shark (right) is a slow swimmer. Its tail is held at a low angle to its midline.

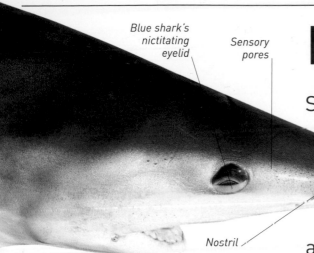

Blue shark's nictitating eyelid

Sensory pores

Nostril

Making sense

Sharks have the same five senses as people – sight, hearing, smell, taste, and touch. They also have a sixth electrical sense, which helps them to locate prey and navigate. Under the water, light levels decrease with depth and sound travels five times faster. Sharks can detect vibrations made by animals moving through the water, giving them the sense called "distant-touch".

Metal detector
Hammerheads hunt for fish in the same way a person uses a metal detector to find buried metal.

Going to its head
The head contains the shark's major sense organs, including the sensory pores that are used to detect weak electrical signals. The eye is partly covered by a protective nictitating (blinking) eyelid. As the shark swims, water flows through its nostrils, bringing a constant stream of odours.

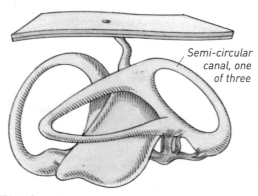

Feeding frenzy
When sharks are feeding on bait, they often snap wildly at their food and bite each other.

Semi-circular canal, one of three

The inner ear
Sharks' ears are inside their heads on either side of the brain case. The three semi-circular canals placed at right angles to each other help the shark to work out which way it has turned in the water. Receptors in the inner ear pick up sounds travelling through the water.

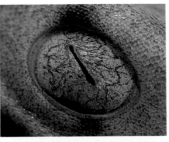

Epaulette's slit-shaped pupil

Dogfish with closed pupil

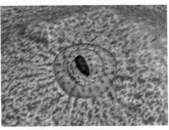

Angel shark's pupil

Reef shark with vertical pupil

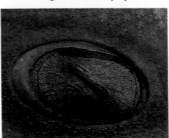

Horn shark's pupil

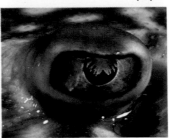

Ray with light-blocking screen

Eyes
In dim light, the pupils in a shark's eye expand to let in as much light as possible. In bright light, they narrow to tiny slits. The eye's retina, where images are focused, contains two types of cells – rods are sensitive to light changes, while cones help with detail and probably allow sharks to see in colour. A special layer of cells called the tapetum helps sharks to see in dim light.

Distant touch
Sharks have a line of special cells along the length of their body, called the lateral line. These cells detect vibrations in the water.

Lateral line

Starry smooth-hound showing lateral line

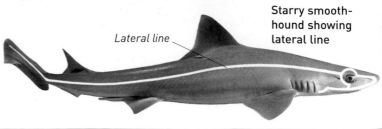

Eyes on stalks

Hammerheads' eyes are set on either side of their head projections, giving them a wide field of vision. The nostrils are widely spaced on the front of the head, helping them detect where a smell is coming from.

Compass

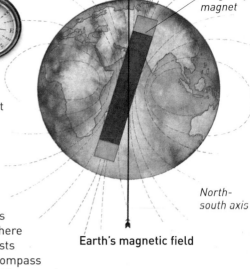

Imaginary magnet

North-south axis

Earth's magnetic field

Compass sense

Some sharks migrate hundreds of kilometres and appear to know where they are going. Scientists think sharks have a "compass sense" to guide them. They may be able to navigate by sensing changes in their own electric fields in relation to the Earth's magnetic field. Corrections have to be made for speed and direction of ocean currents, which could sweep the shark off course.

Duck-billed platypus

Like the shark, the Australian duck-billed platypus can also detect electrical signals from its prey, using receptors on the left-hand side of its bill. Platypuses live in streams, where they hunt for insects and other small creatures.

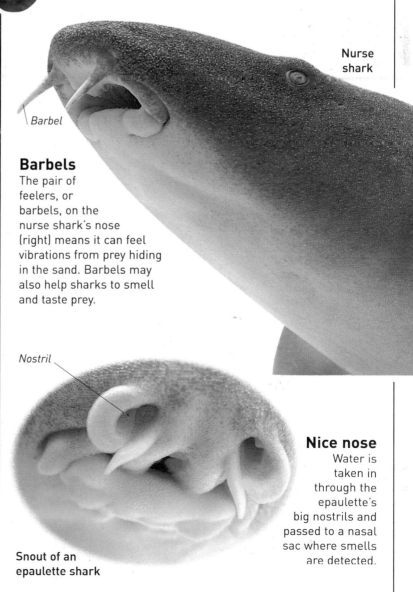

Nurse shark

Barbel

Barbels

The pair of feelers, or barbels, on the nurse shark's nose (right) means it can feel vibrations from prey hiding in the sand. Barbels may also help sharks to smell and taste prey.

Spotty nose

The spots on this sand tiger's snout are sensory pores, called ampullae of Lorenzini. Full of jelly, the pores detect weak electrical signals, helping the shark find prey at close range.

Nostril

Snout of an epaulette shark

Nice nose

Water is taken in through the epaulette's big nostrils and passed to a nasal sac where smells are detected.

Reproduction

Sharks produce young in three ways. Some female sharks are viviparous, which means that they give birth to baby sharks called pups (pp. 22–23). Other sharks are oviparous, which means that they lay eggs in the water. The eggs are encased in a leathery shell and deposited on the sea bed. Once the eggs are laid, the female swims away, leaving them to develop and hatch on their own – just like birds or bony fish. Most sharks, however, are ovoviviparous, which means that the young develop inside eggs but hatch while they are still inside the mother.

Mermaids
Mermaids are mythical creatures with a woman's body and a fish's tail. The empty egg cases of dogfish and rays that wash up on the sea shore are called mermaids' purses.

Spiral egg case
The horn shark wedges its egg case into rocks to protect it.

Holding on
The egg case of the dogfish, or cat shark, is firmly anchored onto anything growing on the sea bed to keep it from being swept away.

Catch me if you can
This male white tip reef shark is chasing a female in the hope that she will mate with him. He may be attracted by her smell.

Keeping close
The male white tip reef shark bites the female to encourage her to mate. He holds her pectoral fin in his jaws to keep her close during mating.

Thick skins
Female blue sharks have much thicker skins than males, so preventing serious injury during courtship.

Mating
People rarely see sharks mating in the wild, or even in aquariums. It seems that larger sharks mate side to side, while smaller male sharks wrap themselves around the female when mating.

Dogfish eggs

Baby dogfish, or embryos, lie safe inside their egg cases, which are anchored onto seaweed by tendrils. The embryos take about nine months to develop before they hatch. During this time, each embryo gets its nourishment from its large yolk sac.

Tendril

Dogfish embryo

Yolk sac

Pair of dogfish egg cases

Pair of ten-day-old dogfish

Cream-coloured underside

Young dogfish

These young dogfish are ten days' old. Although they are only 10 cm (4 in) long, they look like small versions of their parents. Shark pups are generally much larger and more developed than the young of bony fish.

1 One-month-old swell shark embryo

The female swell shark lays two eggs at a time in clumps of seaweed. Each egg is protected by a leathery case. After a month, the egg has developed into a tiny embryo, which draws its nourishment from its large yolk sac.

Colouring consists of light and dark brown bands, with dark spots on shark's top side

2 Embryo at three months old

The embryo now has eyes and a tail. Oxygen in the water passes through the egg case so that the embryo can breathe.

3 Seven-month-old embryo

By now the embryo has a complete set of fins. The baby shark, or pup, will hatch as soon as it has used up the rest of the yolk sac.

4 Two-month-old pup

After ten months, the young swell shark – at 15 cm (6 in) long – has hatched from the egg case. Its mottled colour pattern makes it hard for predators to see where it is hiding on the sea bed.

Two-month-old swell shark pup

Live young

The majority of sharks give birth to live young instead of laying eggs (pp. 20–21). Most female sharks are ovoviviparous, producing large, yolky eggs that develop inside their body. The developing pup, or embryo, is fed by a yolk sac attached to its belly. When this is used up, the pup is ready to be born. In viviparous sharks, such as lemon, blue, bull, and hammerhead sharks, nourishment from the mother's blood passes to the embryo through a tube called the umbilical cord.

Mother and baby
Humans look after their babies, but shark pups must fend for themselves as soon as they are born.

Birth of a lemon shark
(1) Lemon sharks come into shallow coastal lagoons, which are sheltered from the waves, to give birth. The tip of the pup's tail is just visible poking out of its mother.
(2) Here, the female has begun to give birth.
(3) The scientist is helping the pup to pass out of the mother's birth canal.

Hammerheads

Hammerhead sharks can give birth to up to 40 pups at a time. While in the womb, each pup is connected to its mother by an umbilical cord.

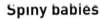

Baby African elephant

A baby elephant takes 22 months to gestate (develop inside its mother's body). The spiny dogfish has a similar gestation period of between 18 and 24 months.

Spiny babies

Just as spines on hedgehog babies emerge after birth, those on baby spiny dogfish have special coverings that protect their mother.

Bigeye thresher pup

As a bigeye thresher pup develops inside the womb, it feeds on eggs produced by its mother.

(4) The lemon shark pup is still attached to its mother by the umbilical cord.
(5) The pup rests on the sea bed, then swims away, breaking the cord.
(6) The pup faces life on it own, hiding from predators in mangrove roots. For many years it will stay in a small nursery area in the lagoon, near where it was born. Then it will make trips out of the lagoon to the coral reefs and further afield.

6

4

5

Gentle giants

Humpback whales
Whale sharks are named after those other ocean giants — the whales.

Whale sharks are the largest fish in the world, reaching lengths of at least 12 m (40 ft) and weighing 13.2 tonnes (14.6 US tons). These harmless giants can cruise at 3 kph (1.9 mph), often near the surface of the water. They live in warm, tropical waters in places where there is a good supply of food to support their large bulk, and feed by filtering food out of the water. Whale sharks give birth to as many as 300 pups, hatched from eggs inside their bodies (pp. 20–23).

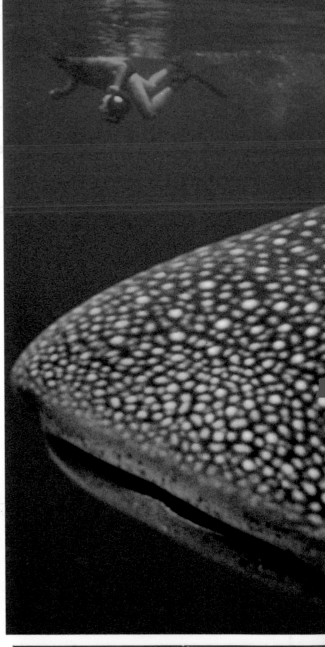

0 2,000 4,000 6,000 km

At the dentist
Humans need to replace lost teeth with false ones in order to chew food.

Not much of a bite
Whale sharks do not bite or chew, so they do not need their tiny teeth.

Distribution of whale sharks

A great gulp
Despite their great size, whale sharks feed on plankton (small plants and animals that drift in the sea), small fish, and squid. As the sea water passes through their huge mouths, food is strained through bristly filters called gill rakers. Other large fish, such as basking sharks (pp. 34–35), manta rays (pp. 8–9), and baleen whales also feed by filtering food out of the water.

White-spotted bamboo sharks grow to about 95 cm (37 in) long

Anal fin

Nurse sharks grow to 3 m (10 ft) long

Brown-banded bamboo sharks grow to just over 1 m (3.3 ft) long

One big happy family

Although they are much smaller, these four sharks (white-spotted and brown-banded bamboos, epaulette, and nurse) all belong to the same group as the whale shark. They all have two barbels on their snouts which help them to find food buried in the sea bed.

Barbel

Epaulette sharks grow to 1 m (3.3 ft) long

Basking beauties

Cruising along with their huge mouths wide open to filter food, basking sharks are like giant mobile sieves. The second largest fish in the world, after the whale shark (pp. 32–33), basking sharks grow to about 10 m (33 ft) long and weigh over 4 tonnes (4.4 US tons). They often swim at the surface on sunny days with their dorsal fins out of the water. Unfortunately, they make easy targets for fishermen who catch them for their large fins, meat, and the oil in their livers – which may be a quarter of the shark's body weight.

Shark fishing
This basking shark was caught at Achill Island off the coast of Ireland. Fishing stopped when the numbers of sharks declined.

Eye

Nostril

Gill arch – water passes through arch and then through a sieve of gill rakers

Oily mouths
Oil from sharks' livers has been used in cosmetics such as lipstick.

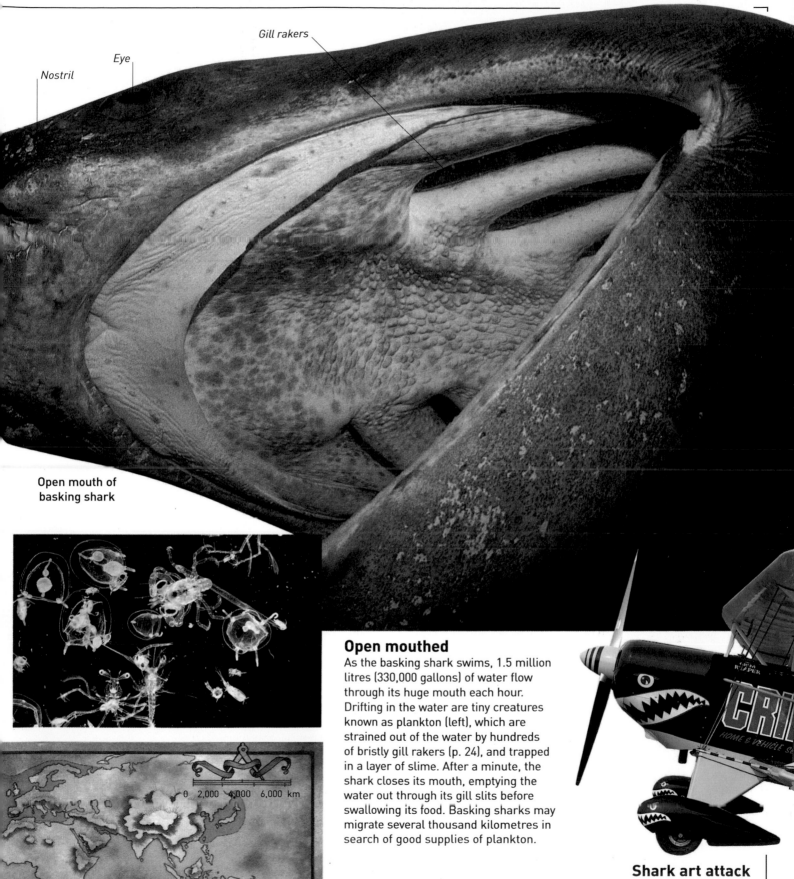

Nostril

Eye

Gill rakers

Open mouth of
basking shark

Open mouthed

As the basking shark swims, 1.5 million litres (330,000 gallons) of water flow through its huge mouth each hour. Drifting in the water are tiny creatures known as plankton (left), which are strained out of the water by hundreds of bristly gill rakers (p. 24), and trapped in a layer of slime. After a minute, the shark closes its mouth, emptying the water out through its gill slits before swallowing its food. Basking sharks may migrate several thousand kilometres in search of good supplies of plankton.

0 2,000 4,000 6,000 km

Distribution
of basking
sharks

Shark art attack

This bi-plane has an eye-catching shark-face design on its nose and tyre covers. During World War II, shark faces were painted on US fighter planes to instill fear in the enemy.

Angel sharks

The 16 species of angel shark have flattened bodies and broad pectoral fins that look like angels' wings. These strange sharks hide on the sea bed waiting to ambush prey with their snapping jaws. Found in shallow coastal waters, angel sharks swim like other sharks using their large tails to propel themselves forward.

Monk fish
Angel sharks are also known as "monk fish", because the shape of their heads looks like the hood on a monk's cloak.

Lower lobe of tail is longer than the upper lobe – a feature unique to angel sharks

Second dorsal fin

0   2,000   4,000   6,000 km

Distribution of angel sharks

Pelvic fin

First dorsal fin

Gill slit

Mouth

Eye

Spiracle

Pelvic fin

Look-alikes
Rays are flat like angel sharks, but their pectoral fins are joined to their head and their gill slits are on the underside of the body.

Underside of ray

Pectoral fin

Top side of ray

Angels
This angel shark grows up to 2 m (6.5 ft) long. It is found in the Mediterranean and Baltic seas, the eastern Atlantic Ocean, and the English Channel. To get oxygen, the angel shark draws in water through the large spiracles on the top of its head. Water drawn through the spiracles is more likely to be free of silt than water taken in through the mouth.

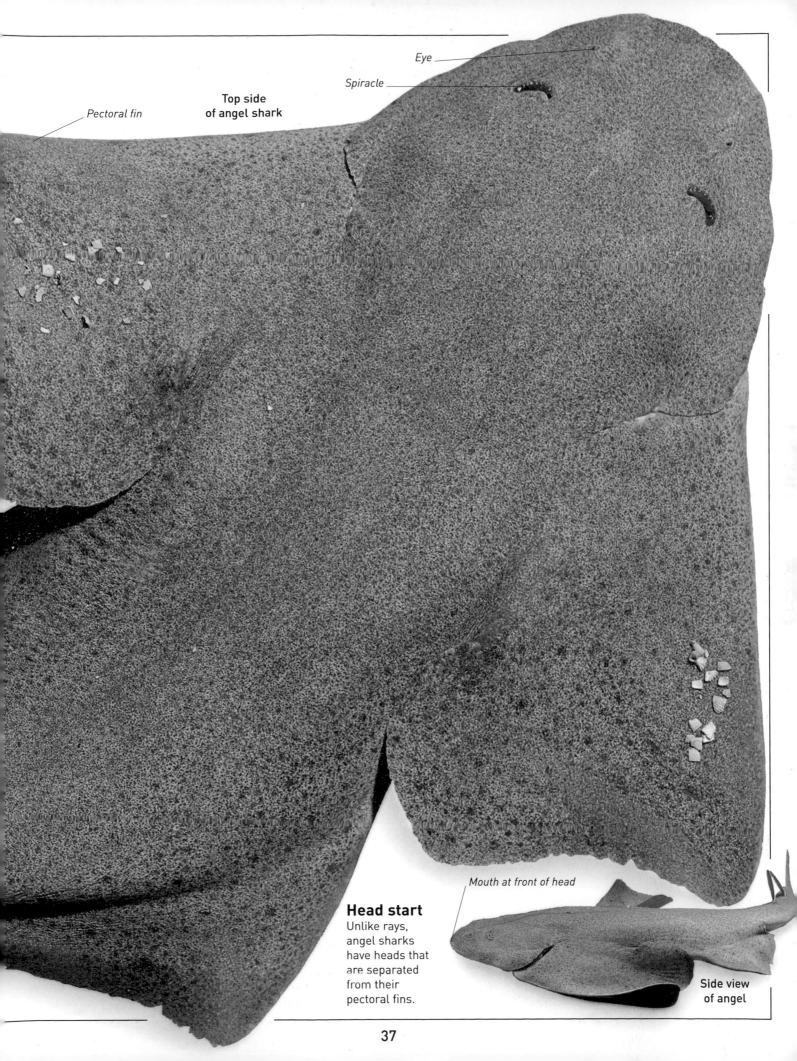

Eye

Spiracle

Top side of angel shark

Pectoral fin

Mouth at front of head

Head start
Unlike rays, angel sharks have heads that are separated from their pectoral fins.

Side view of angel

Japanese wobbegong

Lobe

Barbel

Secret agent
Like undercover spies, some sharks disguise themselves to hide from predators.

Japanese wobbegong
This shark grows to about 1 m (3.3 ft). Wobbegongs are not usually aggressive, but people have been bitten when they have stepped on one by mistake.

Undercover sharks

Many bottom-dwelling sharks use camouflage to help them blend in with their surroundings. They have blotches, spots, or stripes that make them difficult to see on the sea bed. Wobbegongs have blotchy skins and lobes on their heads that look like bits of seaweed. Swell sharks hide in crevices, while angel sharks cover themselves with sand. These undercover sharks often lie in wait for prey to move near, then snap them up. Smaller sharks use camouflage to avoid being eaten by larger predators.

Sand disguise
It is difficult to see angel sharks (pp. 36–37) lying on the sea bed because they are flattened, and their mottled skin looks like sand (top left). To complete their disguise, they shuffle their pectoral fins to bury their bodies in sand (centre left). Their eyes poke above the surface of the sand (bottom left) watching for prey. When a fish comes near, the angel shark lunges forward, snapping its jaws shut around it.

Bearded disguise
The branched lobes around the tasselled wobbegong's mouth look like seaweed to unsuspecting prey.

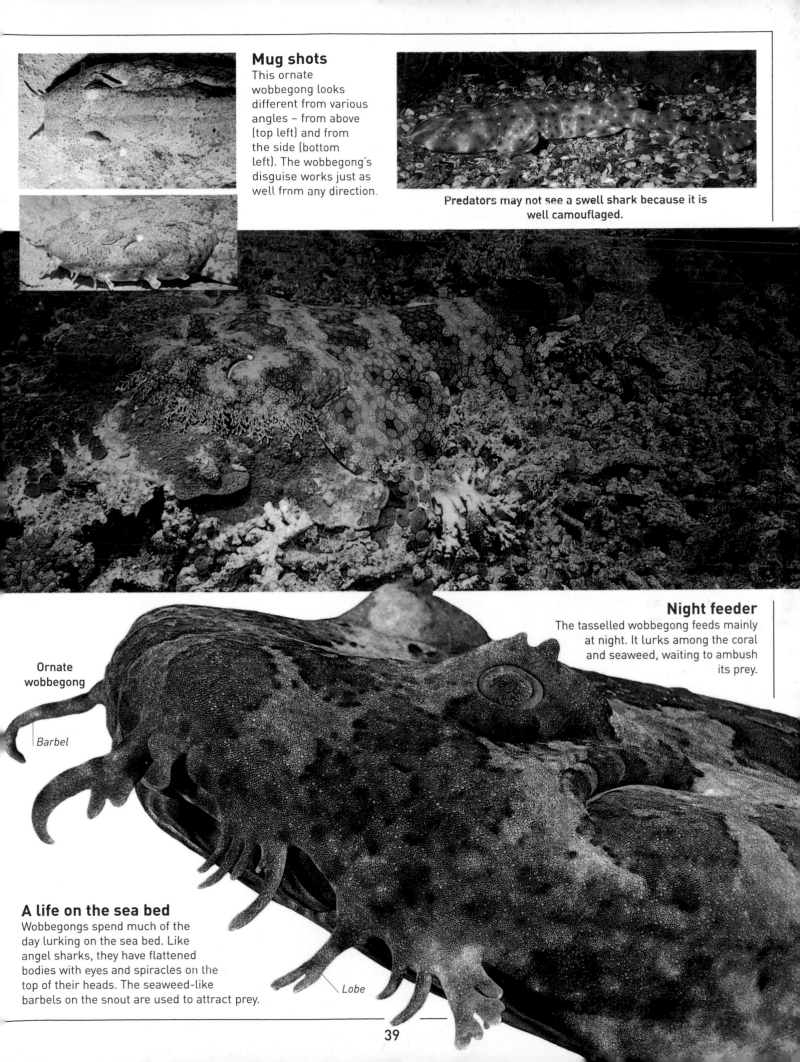

Mug shots
This ornate wobbegong looks different from various angles – from above (top left) and from the side (bottom left). The wobbegong's disguise works just as well from any direction.

Predators may not see a swell shark because it is well camouflaged.

Ornate wobbegong

Barbel

Night feeder
The tasselled wobbegong feeds mainly at night. It lurks among the coral and seaweed, waiting to ambush its prey.

A life on the sea bed
Wobbegongs spend much of the day lurking on the sea bed. Like angel sharks, they have flattened bodies with eyes and spiracles on the top of their heads. The seaweed-like barbels on the snout are used to attract prey.

Lobe

Horn sharks

Horn sharks get their name from the two horn-shaped spines on their backs. They are also known as bullheads because they have broad heads with ridges above the eyes. The nine species of horn shark are found in the Pacific and Indian oceans, where they live on the sea bed in shallow water. They swim with slow beats of their tails and push themselves along the bottom with their pectoral fins. Sadly, horn sharks are often killed for their spines, which are used to make jewellery.

Practising the horn makes perfect

Pelvic fin

A pair of swimming Port Jackson sharks, which are named after a harbour in Australia

Heap of horns

Port Jackson sharks often rest in groups during the day. Favourite rest sites are the sandy floors of caves or the channels between rocks. At night they search for food such as sea urchins and starfish.

Spine in front of first dorsal fin

Caudal (tail) fin

Spine of second dorsal fin

Typical spotted pattern on skin

Eye

Side view of horn shark

Pelvic fin

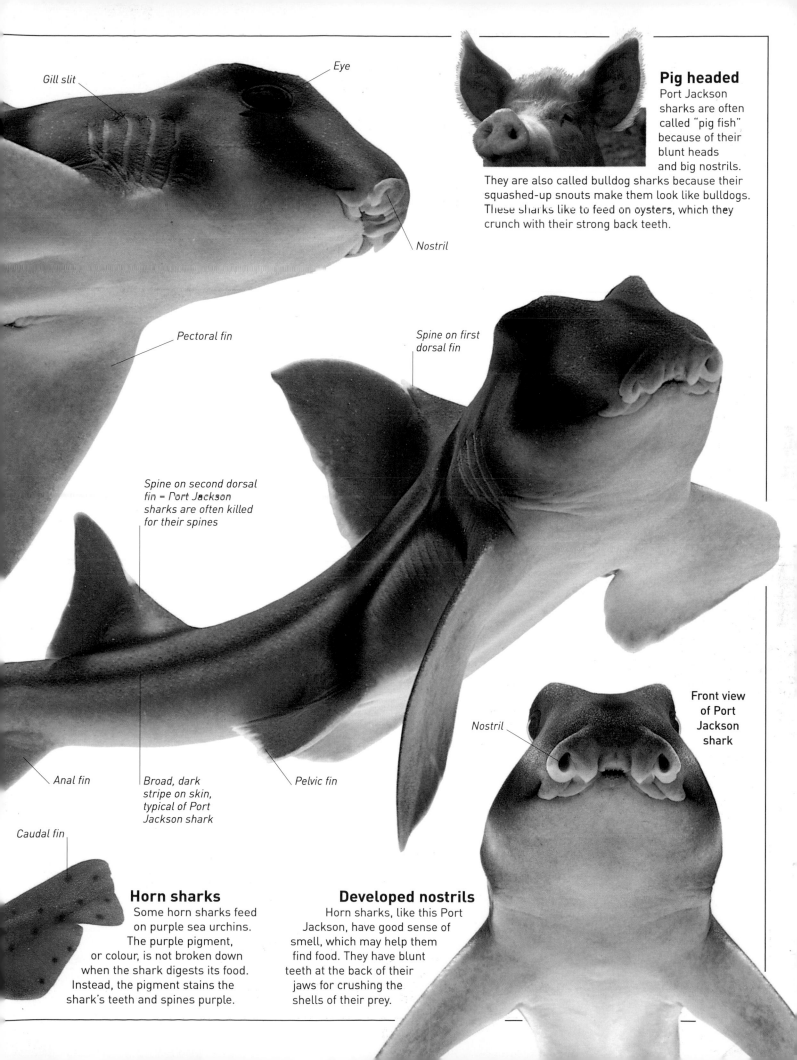

Gill slit

Eye

Pectoral fin

Spine on first
dorsal fin

Nostril

Spine on second dorsal
fin – Port Jackson
sharks are often killed
for their spines

Anal fin

Broad, dark
stripe on skin,
typical of Port
Jackson shark

Pelvic fin

Caudal fin

Nostril

Front view
of Port
Jackson
shark

Pig headed

Port Jackson
sharks are often
called "pig fish"
because of their
blunt heads
and big nostrils.
They are also called bulldog sharks because their
squashed-up snouts make them look like bulldogs.
These sharks like to feed on oysters, which they
crunch with their strong back teeth.

Horn sharks

Some horn sharks feed
on purple sea urchins.
The purple pigment,
or colour, is not broken down
when the shark digests its food.
Instead, the pigment stains the
shark's teeth and spines purple.

Developed nostrils

Horn sharks, like this Port
Jackson, have good sense of
smell, which may help them
find food. They have blunt
teeth at the back of their
jaws for crushing the
shells of their prey.

Hammerheads

Of all the sharks, hammerheads have the strangest shaped heads. The nine species of hammerhead include the bonnetheads and the wingheads, whose heads can grow to half the length of their body. Scalloped hammerheads are found in warm waters throughout the world. They gather in large groups, called schools, around seamounts (underwater mountains or volcanoes).

Distribution of hammerheads

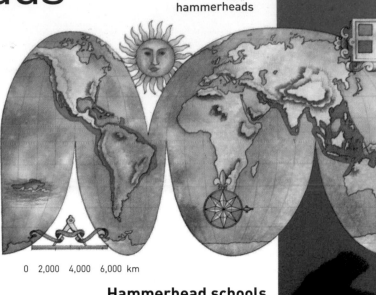

Bonnetheads
Wingheads

0   2,000   4,000   6,000 km

Hammerhead schools

Hammerheads often swim in schools of hundreds of sharks, but the reason why they group together is unclear. These large predators have few enemies, so it is unlikely they gather for protection.

Difficult diet

Stingrays are the favourite food of the great hammerhead, even though their tails are armed with venomous spines, or "stings".

Blue-spotted stingray

Two different sharks

The shape of the hammerhead's head (top) compared to that of other sharks, like the tope (bottom), fascinated early naturalists.

A fine bonnet

Bonnetheads are the smallest of the hammerheads, reaching only 1.5 m (5 ft) long.

Dorsal fin

Gill slit

Mouth

Pectoral fin

Anal fin   *Pelvic fin*

Why a hammer?

No-one knows why a hammerhead has a hammer-shaped head, but the broad, flattened head may give extra lift to the front of the shark's body as it swims.

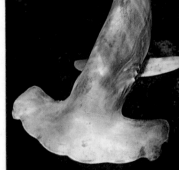

Head on

Hammerheads' eyes are at the tips of their "hammers", giving them an excellent view as they swing their heads from side to side. They also use their ampullae of Lorenzini (p. 19) to help them locate prey.

Scalloped hammerhead

Weird and wonderful

The megamouth, one of the world's most extraordinary sharks, was only discovered in 1976. No-one had seen this large shark before, although it is more than 5 m (16 ft) long and weighs 680 kg (1,500 lb). Since 1976, more than 55 megamouths have been found, including one that was captured alive off the coast of California in 1990. Another strange shark, the goblin shark, lives in deep water and is rarely seen alive. Other mysteries have been solved. No-one knew what caused circular bites on whales, dolphins, and seals, but the culprits were found to be cookiecutter sharks.

Places where the first megamouths were found

Big mouth
Megamouth is named after its huge mouth, which can measure up to 1m (3ft) wide. It feeds on animal plankton, attracting prey with luminous (glowing) organs around its lips. The first megamouth was found entangled in the anchor of a US naval boat off Hawaii.

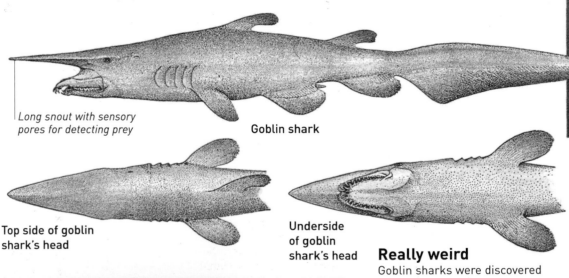

Long snout with sensory pores for detecting prey

Goblin shark

Top side of goblin shark's head

Underside of goblin shark's head

Really weird
Goblin sharks were discovered off the coast of Japan in 1898. They grow to 3 m (10 ft) long and live in deep water down to at least 1,300 m (4,265 ft).

Glows in the dark
The lantern shark (left) lives in the oceans' depths. They are called lantern sharks because they glow in the dark. Among the world's smallest sharks, they grow to only 20 cm (8 in) long.

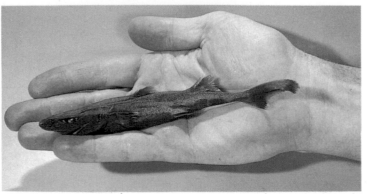

Distribution of cookiecutters

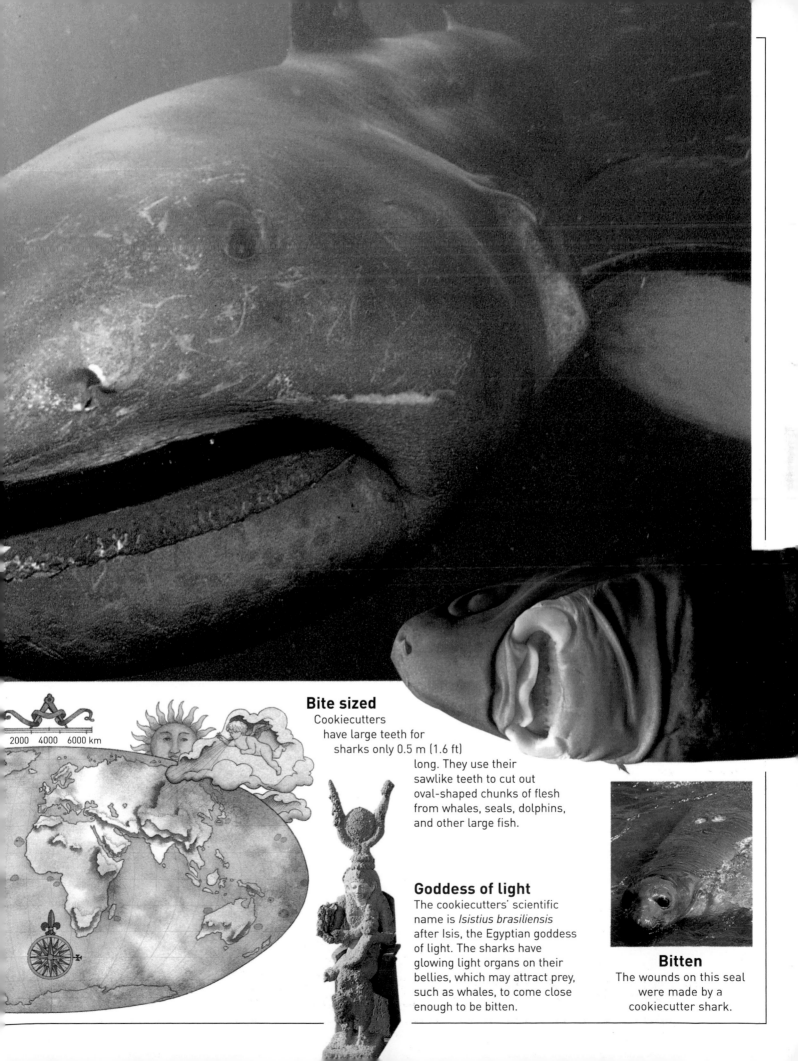

2000 4000 6000 km

Bite sized
Cookiecutters
have large teeth for
sharks only 0.5 m (1.6 ft)
long. They use their
sawlike teeth to cut out
oval-shaped chunks of flesh
from whales, seals, dolphins,
and other large fish.

Goddess of light
The cookiecutters' scientific
name is *Isistius brasiliensis*
after Isis, the Egyptian goddess
of light. The sharks have
glowing light organs on their
bellies, which may attract prey,
such as whales, to come close
enough to be bitten.

Bitten
The wounds on this seal
were made by a
cookiecutter shark.

Shark artefacts

For centuries, people have caught sharks and taken their teeth and skin to make a wide variety of objects, or artefacts. Early people made tools from sharks' teeth, while the skin was used to make shoes and grips for weapons (p. 60). Fishing for sharks with primitive tools was difficult and dangerous, and stories and legends about sharks were common among seafaring people.

Monkey
The teeth of this Mexican monkey head are taken from a shark.

Large, serrated tooth, probably from a great white shark (pp. 28–31)

Tooth necklace
The ten teeth in this decorative necklace probably came from great white sharks caught by Maoris off the coast of New Zealand.

Shark-shaped gold weight from Ghana, West Africa

Shoes made of shark skin, from India

Shark skin

Tin toy from Malaysia

Shark tooth

Shark tooth

Tool, tipped with a shark's tooth

18th-century wooden drum, made with shark skin, from the Hawaiian Islands

Wooden scraper, covered in shark skin, from Santa Cruz in the Pacific

Shark tooth

Shark skin

Shark skin grater (below) from the Wallis Islands in the Pacific

Wooden knife (right) made with sharks' teeth from Greenland

Shark skin

Sharks in the home
From ancient times, the skins and teeth of sharks have been used to make a variety of household items, such as food graters, knives, and tools. The soft skin can be used like leather for making shoes, belts, or even drums (above).

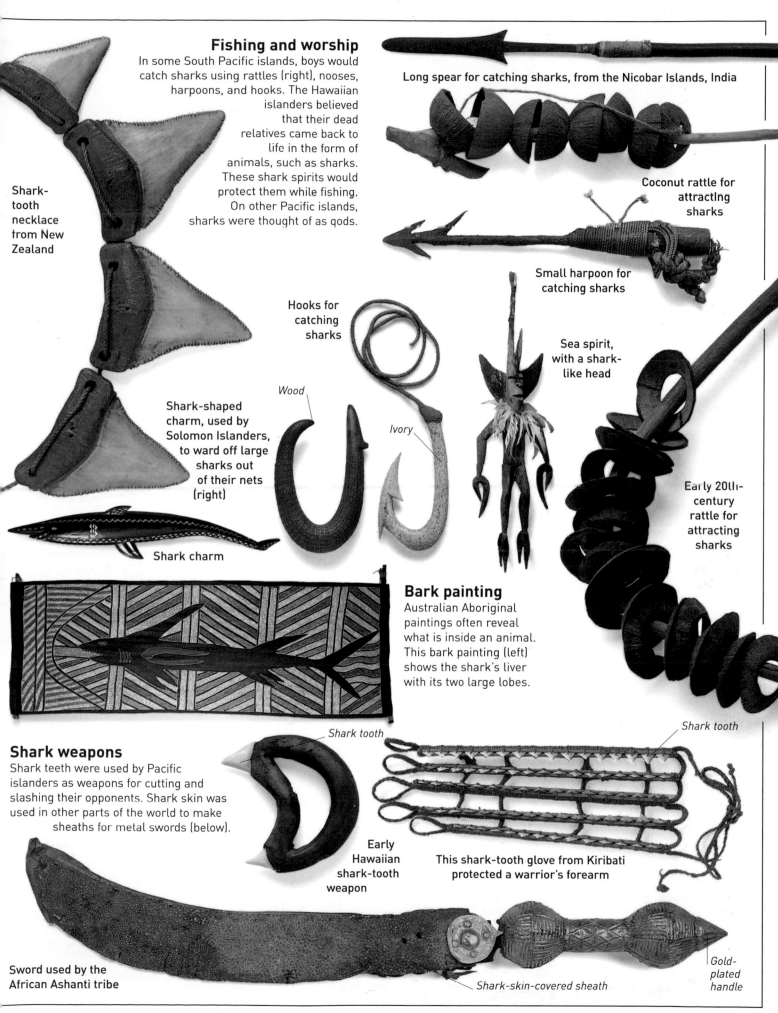

Fishing and worship

In some South Pacific islands, boys would catch sharks using rattles (right), nooses, harpoons, and hooks. The Hawaiian islanders believed that their dead relatives came back to life in the form of animals, such as sharks. These shark spirits would protect them while fishing. On other Pacific islands, sharks were thought of as gods.

Long spear for catching sharks, from the Nicobar Islands, India

Coconut rattle for attracting sharks

Shark-tooth necklace from New Zealand

Small harpoon for catching sharks

Hooks for catching sharks

Wood

Ivory

Sea spirit, with a shark-like head

Shark-shaped charm, used by Solomon Islanders, to ward off large sharks out of their nets (right)

Shark charm

Early 20th-century rattle for attracting sharks

Bark painting

Australian Aboriginal paintings often reveal what is inside an animal. This bark painting (left) shows the shark's liver with its two large lobes.

Shark tooth

Shark weapons

Shark teeth were used by Pacific islanders as weapons for cutting and slashing their opponents. Shark skin was used in other parts of the world to make sheaths for metal swords (below).

Shark tooth

Early Hawaiian shark-tooth weapon

This shark-tooth glove from Kiribati protected a warrior's forearm

Sword used by the African Ashanti tribe

Shark-skin-covered sheath

Gold-plated handle

Shark attack

Attack at sea
Prisoners, escaping from Devil's Island off Guyana, are attacked by sharks.

Most sharks are not dangerous and rarely attack humans. Every year about 75 shark attacks are reported worldwide, with up to ten of these being fatal. It is not safe to be in water where there may be sharks. Take note of the warning signs and do not swim if the sea is murky, if you have cut yourself, or if bait has been put out for fish.

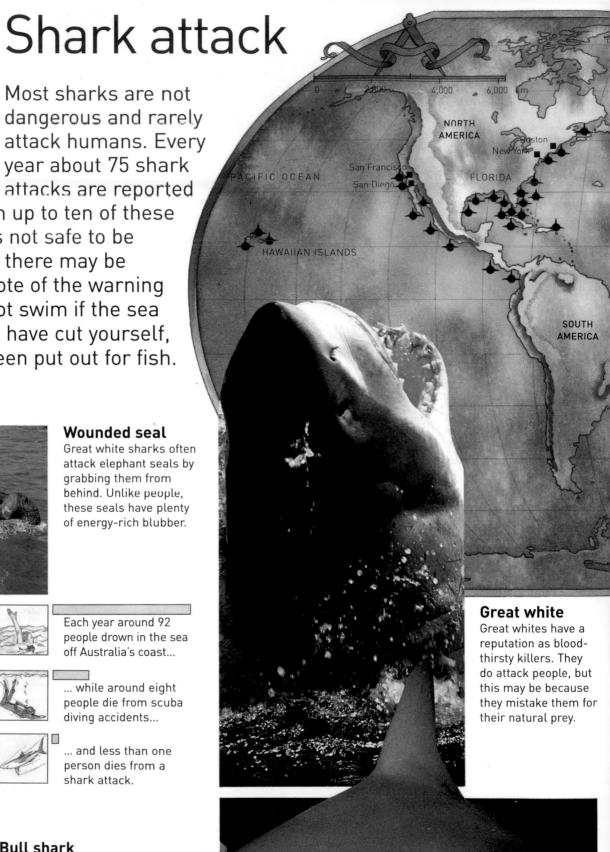

Great white
Great whites have a reputation as blood-thirsty killers. They do attack people, but this may be because they mistake them for their natural prey.

Wounded seal
Great white sharks often attack elephant seals by grabbing them from behind. Unlike people, these seals have plenty of energy-rich blubber.

Fatal attack
Most fatal shark attacks occur where people surf, swim, or scuba dive, and where there are large sharks, like the great white, swimming close to shore.

 Each year around 92 people drown in the sea off Australia's coast...

 ... while around eight people die from scuba diving accidents...

 ... and less than one person dies from a shark attack.

Warning sign
Read the warning signs as sharks often attack people in shallow water.

Bull shark
Bull sharks are one of the most dangerous sharks in the world, along with great whites and tiger sharks. The bull shark is one of the few sharks that swims in freshwater lakes and rivers.

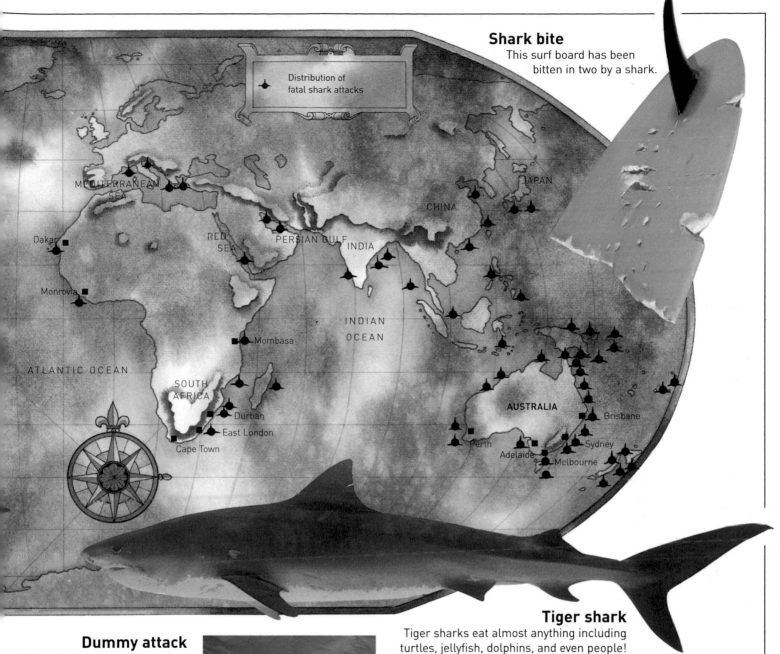

Shark bite
This surf board has been bitten in two by a shark.

Distribution of fatal shark attacks

MEDITERRANEAN SEA

Dakar

Monrovia

RED SEA

PERSIAN GULF

INDIA

CHINA

JAPAN

INDIAN OCEAN

ATLANTIC OCEAN

SOUTH AFRICA

Mombasa

Durban
East London
Cape Town

AUSTRALIA

Brisbane

Perth

Adelaide

Sydney

Melbourne

Tiger shark
Tiger sharks eat almost anything including turtles, jellyfish, dolphins, and even people!

Dummy attack
Wet suits do not protect against shark attacks as this experiment with a dummy shows.

Shark's eye view
Sharks can mistake surfers for seals because they have similar shapes when seen from below.

Grey reef shark
When swimming normally, the back of a grey reef shark is gently curved and the pectoral fins are held straight.

Threat posture
If threatened, the grey reef will arch its back and hold its pectoral fins downwards. It may also swim in a figure of eight.

Sharks at bay

There is no simple way to protect people from sharks. Shark-proof enclosures can protect only small areas because they are expensive. In South Africa and Australia, nets are used along popular beaches to trap sharks, but they also catch harmless sharks, dolphins, rays, and turtles. Some countries use drumlines (baited lines with hooks). Other methods include magnetic, electrical, and chemical repellents. If a shark does become aggressive, punching or kicking its snout may put it off an attack.

Jonah
Jonah, in the Bible story, may have been swallowed by a shark, rather than a whale.

Life guards
If sharks are spotted near a beach, a shark alarm is sounded and swimmers must leave the water.

Shark Shield
The Shark Shield repels sharks by generating an electric field.

In the bag
The US Navy found that sharks avoided people in inflatable bags because they could not see any limbs, sense any electrical signals, or smell blood or body wastes.

Trapped
In the 1930s, more than 1,500 sharks were caught in mesh nets. Since then, the numbers of sharks have decreased sharply.

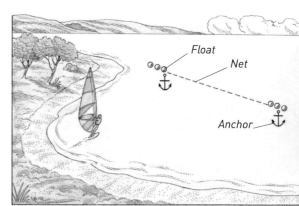

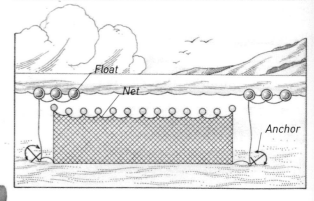

Netting beaches
Mesh nets are used to trap sharks near popular beaches. The nets do not form a continuous barrier, so sharks may be caught on either side of the net. Heavy anchors keep the nets on the sea bed, and floats keep the top of the net suspended in the water. The nets are checked each day and dead sea animals are removed. After three weeks the nets need to be replaced as they become covered in seaweed and other marine growth, and so can easily be seen and avoided by sharks.

Chain wall

This wall of interlinked chains surrounding an Australian beach stops sharks from getting in. These walls are too costly to protect more than a few kilometres of beach.

Protected beach

Of all the methods used to deter sharks, nets such as this one in Australia (above) seem to offer the best protection.

Invisible barrier

Here, an invisible electrical barrier is being tested. When the current is off (top) the shark swims past, but when the current is switched on (left) the shark turns back to avoid it.

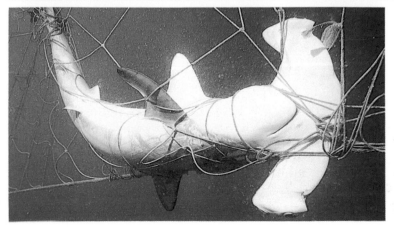

Death nets

Mesh nets, used to protect beaches, kill many sharks each year, like the great white (above) and hammerhead (left). Sharks caught in nets are not able to swim and suffocate because they cannot keep water flowing over their gills.

Shark repellent

If attacked, the Moses sole from the Red Sea releases a milky liquid from pores on its skin, causing the shark to spit it out.

Filming sharks

Diving suit
In the 19th century, divers wore helmets and had air pumped down tubes from the surface.

Diving with predatory sharks such as the great white (pp. 28–31) can be dangerous, so underwater film-makers and photographers use strong metal cages to protect themselves. With less dangerous species such as the blue shark (pp. 56–57), divers sometimes wear chain-mail suits which prevent the shark's teeth from piercing the skin. When sharks are being filmed outside a cage, safety divers should also be present to look for sharks approaching from outside the film-maker's field of vision.

1 Lowering the cage
Bait is thrown in the water to attract great whites. The metal cage is then lowered into the sea.

2 A great white approaches
It may be several days before a great white comes close to the cage, which is kept on the surface by floats.

3 A view from inside the cage
Baits, like horse meat and tuna, attract the shark to the cage. The bars are close enough together to prevent the shark from biting the diver.

Shining armour
Australian film-makers Ron and Valerie Taylor are well known for their work on sharks. Valerie (left) is testing the effectiveness of a chain-mail suit. The suits are heavy, so swimming is difficult. The blue shark is tempted to bite because the suit's sleeve contains pieces of fish. Butchers also use chain-mail gloves (top) to protect their hands when slicing up meat.

Film-makers
Ron Taylor films a whitetip reef shark taking a bait (right), while a blue shark approaches the camera (below right).

4 Great white swims by
Divers can be shaken off their feet if the great white bumps into the cage. Close-up views show just how big these sharks are.

Studying sharks

HMS Challenger
19th-century naturalists travelled on this British research ship to study sharks.

To find out more about sharks, scientists attach electronic tags to their fins to monitor their movement and behaviour. Great care is taken to keep sharks alive when they are caught for tagging and other studies. Certain types of shark are placed in aquariums for observation (p. 62).

Tracking by satellite
By tracking sharks, scientists have discovered that the great white swims long distances each year.

Seabed retriever

Lemon sharks
US scientist Dr Samuel Gruber has studied lemon sharks for more than ten years. Lemon sharks do not need to swim to breathe, so they can be kept still during observations. A substance is being injected into the shark (right) to show how fast it can grow.

Propeller measuring swimming speed is attached to fin of a mako shark

Water flow
Dr Gruber checks the flow of water through this nurse shark's nose. Nurse sharks are normally docile but they can give a nasty bite.

Scientists' favourite
Lemon sharks are one of the easiest sharks to study. This young lemon shark (left) shakes her head while eating, creating large amounts of debris in the water.

Tagging tigers
Scientists tag a small tiger shark (top). A diver (above) pushes a tiger shark after tagging to keep water flowing over its gills.

Keeping dry
In the 1930s, US naturalist Prof W. Beebe used a vessel called a bathysphere to reach a depth of 1,000 m (3,300 ft).

Frilled sharks
Three of these strange sharks were caught during the 1870s' *Challenger* trip.

Frilled shark

Extra gill slit

Tagging sharks

Fishermen can help scientists find out where sharks go and how fast they grow by measuring, tagging, and releasing them. Tens of thousands of sharks have been tagged since the 1950s. Blue sharks are among the greatest ocean travellers. One tagged near New York was recaptured 16 months later off Brazil, 6,000 km (3,728 miles) away.

Australian certificate and card for details of captured shark

Two tag applicators

Return address

Tag

Metal tip pierces shark's skin

Where blue sharks have been tagged, released, and recaptured

Cornwall, UK

West Africa

Eastern Seaboard, USA

0   1,000   2,000   3,000 km

Bird ringing
Ringing bands around young birds' legs gives information on migration – just as tags do for sharks.

Bait

1 Tagging sharks
Like most sharks, blue sharks have an excellent sense of smell and are attracted to bait. Here, the shark hooks are baited with fresh mackerel, then the fishing lines are let out to depths of 12–18 m (40–59 ft).

2 Hooked
The shark takes the bait.

3 Reeling in

The shark is reeled in carefully.

6 Tagging the fin

The tag is made of strong metal that will not disintegrate in sea water and cause the plastic numbered tag to drop out. On the back is an address to where the tag can be sent if the shark is later recaptured.

Blue flags show two sharks were released

7 Releasing

Holding the tail, the skipper gently lowers the shark back into the sea.

5 Holding the shark down

The skipper holds the female shark down. He has to work quickly to insert the tag into her dorsal fin as the shark cannot survive long out of the water. Buckets of salt water are thrown onto the shark to keep her alive.

4 Threshing shark

The threshing shark is hauled in.

Overkill

People kill sharks for their meal, fins, skin, and liver oil, as well as for sport. But the biggest threat to sharks is overfishing. Compared to bony fish, sharks have a slow rate of reproduction and take a long time to mature. If too many are killed, their numbers may never recover. Efforts are now being made to protect sharks by creating reserves, restricting numbers caught, and banning fishing.

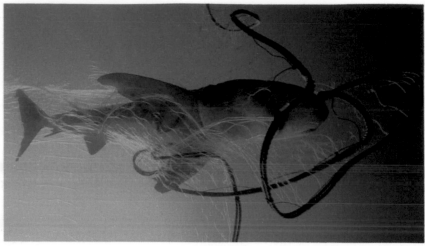

Angling
Angling (fishing) is a popular sport. Today, many angling clubs are restricting the size of shark that can be landed.

Walls of death
Drift nets (top), some 15 m (50 ft) deep and many kilometres long, are used to catch fish. The nets are so fine that sharks do not see them and become trapped in the mesh.

White death
For many anglers, the great white (above) is the ultimate trophy. In many countries hunting these sharks is banned. International trade in shark body parts, such as teeth and jaws, is also controlled.

Sport?
To show just how many sharks were killed, this hunter's boat (left) displays a collection of the victims' jaws.

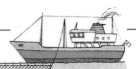

Drift net

Thrashed thresher
Thresher sharks (left) are heavily fished in the Pacific and Indian Oceans. Landing a thresher can be dangerous, especially if they lash out with their tails.

Sad end for a tiger
This tiger shark (right) was killed in an angling competition. Anglers are now encouraged to tag and release the sharks they catch.

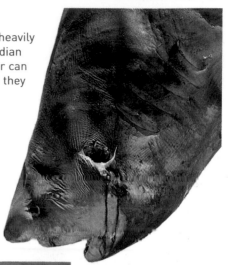

Cutting up sharks for meat

Fishing for food
In developing countries, people depend on shark meat for protein. In other countries, shark is a luxury food. It is important that shark fishing is controlled as many species are at risk of becoming extinct.

Finning
These Japanese fishermen are cutting the fins off sharks caught in drift nets. They throw the rest of the shark back in the sea. Without fins, sharks are not able to swim properly and may be torn apart by other sharks.

Drying fins
Shark-fin soup is a delicacy in the Far East. Because the fins can be dried, they are much easier to market than shark meat, which has to be sold quickly.

Shark fins drying

Use and abuse

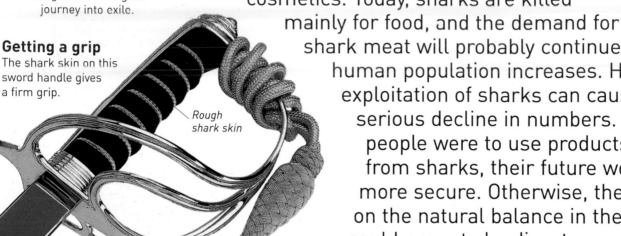

Shark teeth
These pendants are made from the teeth of a great white shark.

People have found a use for almost every part of a shark's body. The skin can be turned into leather, the teeth into jewellery, and the oil from the liver used in industry, medicines, and cosmetics. Today, sharks are killed mainly for food, and the demand for shark meat will probably continue as the human population increases. Human exploitation of sharks can cause a serious decline in numbers. If fewer people were to use products made from sharks, their future would be more secure. Otherwise, the effect on the natural balance in the oceans could prove to be disastrous.

Napoleon
The French emperor Napoleon (1769–1821) watches a shark being killed during his journey into exile.

Getting a grip
The shark skin on this sword handle gives a firm grip.

Rough shark skin

The shark skin on the handle of this British officer's sword has been dyed

Rough ray skin under black cord

Samurai sword
This 19th-century sword covered in ray skin belonged to a Samurai warrior from Japan.

Lacquered ray-skin-covered sheath

Curved ivory handle

Persian dagger
The sheath of this 19th-century Persian dagger is covered in lacquered ray skin.

Box of happiness
Fine shark skin was used to cover this early 20th-century box from Korea. The leather is smooth because the denticles (p. 7) have been highly polished, then lacquered, and dyed dark green.

Outside of each door decorated with double happiness characters

Shark remains
These two hammerheads (pp. 42–43) were caught off the coast of Mexico. Their meat was probably used for food and their skin for leather goods, such as belts and wallets.

Shark and chips
Much of the fish sold in British fish and chip shops is, in fact, spiny dogfish (p. 23), one of the most heavily fished sharks. Sadly, shark steaks are becoming a fashionable delicacy in many restaurants worldwide.

Jaws for sale
In the past, shark jaws were sold to tourists as souvenirs. The sale of great white shark jaws is now banned in many countries.

Headless corpse
This shark was killed for sport and its head was cut off so the jaws could be removed. Shark jaws are popular trophies among hunters.

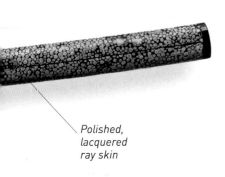

Polished, lacquered ray skin

Shark liver oil pills
Some people take shark liver oil pills to obtain vitamin A, but this vitamin can now be made artificially.

A cluster of shark liver oil pills

Two bowls and a tin of shark fin soup

Shark fin soup
The fibres in shark fins can be made into soup, which some people regard as a delicacy. The dried fins are soaked and repeatedly boiled to extract the fibres.

Skin care
Shark oil is used in costly skin creams. But other creams based on natural plant oils are just as effective.

Save the shark!

Mad on sharks
This sculpture of a blue shark on the roof of a house near Oxford, UK, shows just how much some people like sharks.

Sharks have a bad reputation as blood-thirsty killers. But only a few kinds of shark are dangerous and attacks on people are rare. Sharks are increasingly threatened by overfishing (pp. 58–59). Some sharks, such as lemon sharks in Florida, USA, also suffer because of the loss of mangrove swamps, which are important nurseries for their pups. People can learn more about sharks by visiting an aquarium. Good swimmers can learn to snorkel and scuba dive, and may be lucky enough to see sharks in the sea.

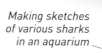
Making sketches of various sharks in an aquarium

Tanks for the view

Seeing sharks at close range is a great thrill. However, not all kinds of shark can be kept in an aquarium. Smaller sharks, such as smooth-hounds (pp. 14–15) are the easiest, but many aquariums are introducing more unusual species. The Okinawa Churaumi Aquarium in Japan keeps whale sharks, and young great white sharks are sometimes kept in the Monterey Bay Aquarium in California, USA.

Face to face with a shark (right) and feeding time at the aquarium (far right)

Recording skate and ray egg cases

Certain kinds of ray and skate are also under threat. The UK-based charity, the Shark Trust, encourages people to record empty skate and ray egg cases that wash up on beaches. This may give clues as to the whereabouts of skate and ray nursery grounds.

Learning about sharks

Join a conservation group that works to protect marine life. Look out for wildlife magazines and books about sharks. There are also interesting underwater programmes on television which, unlike the scary *Jaws* movies, tell the real story about sharks.

A sketch of a classic requiem shark, with its streamlined body

A typical mackerel shark

Sketching sharks can be fun as well as useful

Sharks on file

Visiting aquariums, keeping a notebook, and drawing pictures of sharks are good ways of seeing how many different kinds of sharks there are. Compare the sharks' colours, skin patterns, and different body shapes. Note down the size, diet, natural habitat, and how the various sharks differ. With some effort, anyone can become more of an expert on sharks.

Noting down your observations can help build up a shark information file

Pastels

Pencils

Did you know?

FASCINATING FACTS

Natives of some Pacific islands once worshipped sharks as gods, and therefore would never eat their meat.

Sharks have a large heart with four separate chambers.

Sharks often have very powerful jaws; some are capable of exerting 60 kg (132 lb) of pressure per tooth when they bite.

Great white shark's tooth

Tiger shark's jaw

The spiral valve in a shark's intestine provides a relatively large surface area in a limited space. It slows up digestion considerably, though, so a meal can take anything up to four days to digest.

Galapagos shark

The Galapagos shark lives mainly around tropical reefs, but may swim long distances between islands.

When a shark dart is fired into a shark, it releases carbon dioxide, causing the shark to float to the surface and die.

Boat builders in some parts of Africa rub the wood of a new vessel with hammerhead oil in the belief that it will ensure successful voyages.

A shark has an extremely stretchy, U-shaped stomach that can expand to accommodate an enormous meal that will last the animal several days.

A large part of a shark's brain is linked to its sense of smell; sharks can detect one part of scent in 10 billion parts of water.

Tiger sharks' teeth are strong enough to crunch through a turtle's bones and shell.

About 38 million sharks are caught each year for the fin trade.

Shark skin is twice as durable as conventional leather.

Hawksbill turtle

Model of cladoselache, an ancient shark

Since they first appeared millions of years ago, sharks have probably changed less in evolutionary terms than any other vertebrate (back-boned animal).

In 17th-century France, shark brain was eaten to ease the pain of childbirth. It was also combined with white wine and taken for kidney stones.

On average a shark can survive on 0.5– 3 per cent of its body weight per day.

Giving his work the title *The Physical Impossibility of Death in the Mind of Someone Living*, UK artist Damien Hirst exhibited an Australian tiger shark preserved in green embalming fluid inside a steel and glass tank.

Bite marks from cookiecutter sharks were discovered on the rubber coating of listening devices on submarines belonging to the US Navy.

The meat of sharks is still widely eaten (such as dogfish and even porbeagles) but that of the Greenland shark is inedible until left to rot. It is a delicacy in Iceland despite a strong flavour of ammonia.

Upper tail (caudal) lobe

Apart from people, a shark's greatest enemy is another shark; most sharks will happily eat any members of their own species.

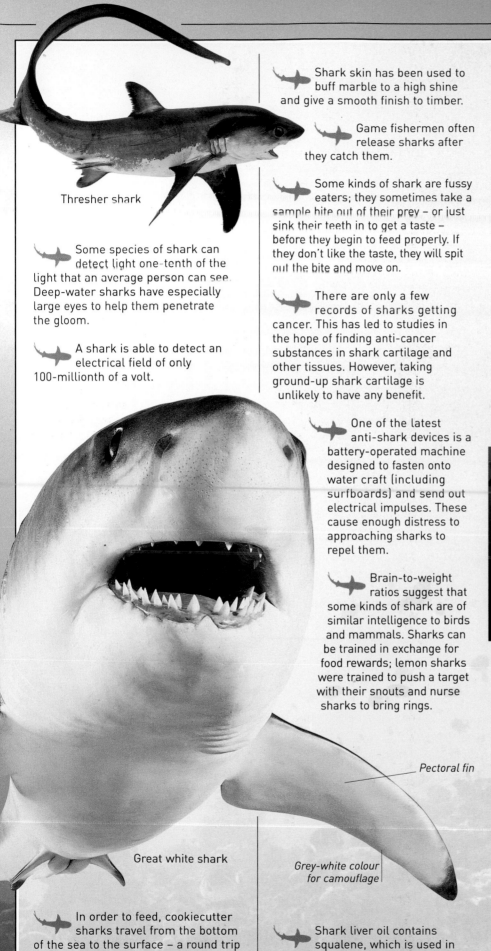

Thresher shark

Some species of shark can detect light one-tenth of the light that an average person can see. Deep-water sharks have especially large eyes to help them penetrate the gloom.

A shark is able to detect an electrical field of only 100-millionth of a volt.

Shark skin has been used to buff marble to a high shine and give a smooth finish to timber.

Game fishermen often release sharks after they catch them.

Some kinds of shark are fussy eaters; they sometimes take a sample bite out of their prey – or just sink their teeth in to get a taste – before they begin to feed properly. If they don't like the taste, they will spit out the bite and move on.

There are only a few records of sharks getting cancer. This has led to studies in the hope of finding anti-cancer substances in shark cartilage and other tissues. However, taking ground-up shark cartilage is unlikely to have any benefit.

One of the latest anti-shark devices is a battery-operated machine designed to fasten onto water craft (including surfboards) and send out electrical impulses. These cause enough distress to approaching sharks to repel them.

Brain-to-weight ratios suggest that some kinds of shark are of similar intelligence to birds and mammals. Sharks can be trained in exchange for food rewards; lemon sharks were trained to push a target with their snouts and nurse sharks to bring rings.

Great white shark

Pectoral fin

Grey-white colour for camouflage

In order to feed, cookiecutter sharks travel from the bottom of the sea to the surface – a round trip of up to 7 km (4.4 miles).

Shark liver oil contains squalene, which is used in cosmetics and alternative medicine.

Reef sharks feeding on surgeon fish

When there's a large quantity of food available, sharks will gather round it in a feeding frenzy, during which they will bite anything that comes near, including each other.

In some shark species, the female continues to produce eggs when she's pregnant, and the developing sharks eat them.

The hammerhead's mouth is located under its head.

Hammerhead shark

The hammerhead shark eats stingrays, swallowing them whole in spite of their poisonous spine.

Sharks prefer to prey on injured or diseased weakened creatures than on strong ones who will fight back. Sharks will also eat dead fish. The great white sometimes feasts on whale carcasses.

Sharks can mistake reflections from metal or sparkly stones for fish scales. Avoid wearing jewellery when you're swimming where sharks have been seen!

Artificial skin from shark cartilage has been used to treat burns.

QUESTIONS AND ANSWERS

Pack of reef sharks hunting at night

Q How can swimmers lessen their chances of attack?

A Sharks tend to attack people who are swimming on their own, so bathers should always stay in a group. They should also avoid waters where seals, sea lions, or large schools of fish are often seen, since sharks are attracted to these creatures. People who are bleeding, even from a small cut anywhere on their body, should remain on the beach, since sharks can sense even the tiniest amount of blood in the water. They are also very sensitive to bodily waste, so it's dangerous to use the sea as a toilet.

Q Do sharks exist together in social relationships?

A Species such as the white tip reef shark are known to hunt in groups. Great white sharks are sometimes found in pairs and small groups at feeding sites where larger sharks appear to dominate the smaller sharks.

Q Are sharks territorial?

A Most sharks do not stay in the same place, but wander freely through the seas. However, some species, such as grey reef sharks, establish a base and patrol it regularly. Similarly, whitetip sharks often stay in the same area for extended periods of time, but they are not known to defend their chosen territory.

Q In what conditions is a shark attack on a person most likely to occur?

A The majority of shark attacks occur where people like to paddle and swim. This is often during the summer months when the water may be warmer. Attacks are most likely to take place in less than 2 m (6 ft 6 in) of calm water, and within a comparatively short distance of the water's edge – about 10 m (35 ft). Particularly hazardous locations are protected inlets, channels where the water suddenly gets deeper, places where rubbish is dumped, and the immediate area around docks, quays, and wharfs, especially where people fish.

Seals can attract hungry sharks and so should be avoided by swimmers.

Q Is each different species of shark known by the same name in every part of the world?

A The common names for sharks can vary widely. The bull shark has a great variety of names, perhaps because it is found in several different habitats. It is known as the Zambezi river shark, Lake Nicaragua shark, Ganges river shark, shovel-nose shark, slipway grey shark, square-nose shark, and Van Rooyen's shark.

Q Are sharks ever found in fresh water?

A Most sharks live in the sea but the bull shark, or Zambezi river shark, may swim into estuaries and up rivers, and is sometimes found in lakes. As a result it comes into closer contact with humans than other sharks. The bull shark is a large predator that sometimes attacks humans.

Bull shark or Zambezi river shark

Shark encounter

A clear observation tunnel at the Sydney Aquarium allows visitors to feel as if they are strolling along the ocean floor. Many aquariums exhibit large sharks such as sand tigers and nurse sharks. Even whale sharks are on show in Japan and the USA.

Fossil teeth one-quarter of their real sizes.

Megalodon tooth

Great white tooth

USEFUL WEBSITES

- UK-based conservation organization dedicated to protecting the world's sharks
  www.sharktrust.org
- The International Shark Attack File
  www.flmnh.ufl.edu/fish
- Official website of the Sydney Aquarium
  www.sydneyaquarium.com.au
- Official website of the London Aquarium
  www.visitsealife.com/london
- Official website of the Monterey Bay Aquarium
  www.montereybayaquarium.org
- Useful website with good information on the biology of sharks and rays
  www.elasmo-research.org
- Gives profiles of different species of shark
  www.sharks-world.com

Leopard shark

PLACES TO VISIT

SEA LIFE SYDNEY AQUARIUM, AUSTRALIA

Located in Darling Harbour, this outstanding exhibition includes:
- a stunning open-ocean display where sharks can be observed at close range
- more than 11,000 aquatic creatures in their natural environment.

SEA LIFE LONDON AQUARIUM, UK

This aquarium has a number of unusual displays, such as:
- separate features on the Atlantic, Pacific, and Indian oceans
- tours and shark feeds.

WAIKIKI AQUARIUM, HAWAII, USA

Shark enthusiasts will be particularly interested in:
- Shark Cam, which keeps a constant watch on the Hunters on the Reef exhibit so the habits and behaviour of the creatures involved (rays, snappers, jacks, and groupers, as well as sharks) can be studied closely.

NATURAL HISTORY MUSEUM OF LOS ANGELES, USA

This museum contains more than 33 million specimens and related artefacts. Shark buffs will not want to miss:
- the rare megamouth shark, first of its species to be exhibited in a museum, and the eleventh to be found since the shark's discovery in 1976.

MONTEREY BAY AQUARIUM, USA

This inspirational aquarium located on the coast of California features:
- a wealth of displays, talks, and sharks on show
- a live web cam of sharks.

THE DEEP, HULL, UK

This wonder of modern architecture includes:
- a ten-metre-deep tank containing nurse, sand tiger, and zebra sharks.

NATIONAL MARINE AQUARIUM, PLYMOUTH, UK

This aquarium houses several different kinds of shark:
- see sharks and exhibits on local and exotic marine life.

Early coconut-shell rattle for attracting sharks, from Samoa in the South Pacific

Index

Acknowledgements

Dorling Kindersley would like to thank the following:
Alan Hills, John Williams, & Mike Row of the British Museum, Harry Taylor & Tim Parmenter of the Natural History Museum, Michael Dent, & Michael Pitts (Hong Kong) for additional special photography; the staff of Sea Life Centres (UK), especially Robin James & Ed Speight (Weymouth) & Rod Haynes (Blackpool), David Bird (Poole Aquarium), & Ocean Park Aquarium (Hong Kong), for providing specimens for photography & species information; the staff of the British Museum, Museum of Mankind, the Natural History Museum, especially Oliver Crimmen of the Fish Dept, the Marine Biological Association (UK), the Marine Conservation Society (UK), Sarah Powler of the Nature Conservation Bureau (UK), the Sydney Aquarium (Darling Harbour, Australia), John West of the Aust. Shark Attack File (Taronga Zoo, Australia), George Burgess of the International Shark Attack File (Florida Museum of Natural History, USA), Dr Peter Klimley (University of California, USA), & Rolf Williams for their research help; Djutja Djutja Munuyngurr, Djapu artist, 1983/1984, tor bark painting; John Reynolds & the Ganesha (Cornwall) for the tagging sequence; Oliver Denton & Carly Nicolls as photographic models; Peter Bailey, Katie Davis (Australia), Muffy Dodson (Hong Kong), Chris Howson, Earl Neish, Manisha Patel, & Helena Spiteri for their design & editorial assistance; Jane Parker for the index; Julie Ferris for proofreading.

Maps: Sallie Alane Reason.
Illustrations: John Woodcock.
Wallchart: Neville Graham, Sue Nicholson, and Susan St. Louis.

For this relaunch edition, the publisher would also like to thank: Hazel Beynon for text editing, and Carron Brown for proofreading.

The publisher would like to thank the following for their kind permission to reproduce their photographs: a=above t=top b=bottom/below c=centre l=left r= right

Ardea: Mark Heiches 52bl; D Parer & E Parer-Cook 19tc; Peter Sleyn 8b, 30bc; Ron & Val Taylor 7br, 38bl, 40cl, 41tr, 49ct, 52t, 52bc, 53tr, 53cr; Valerie Taylor 19bl, 31, 51c, 51bl, 60tr; Wardene Weisser 8c. **Aviation Picture Library /** Austin J Brown 35br. **BBC Natural History Unit:** Michael Pitts 64ca; Jeff Rotman 65tr, 66cla, 66bc, 67cla, 67cr. **The British Museum/ Museum of Mankind:** 46tl, 68bl, 69br. **Bridgeman:** The Prado (Madrid), The Tooth Extractor by Theodor Rombouts (1597–1637), 32bl; Private Collection, The Little Mermaid by E S Hardy, 21tl. **Corbis:** Will Burgess/Reuters 50cla; Paul A Souders 68–69. **Capricorn Press Pty:** 56tl, 56tr. **J Allan Cash:** 27br, 50tr, 51tlb. **Bruce Coleman Ltd:** 59c. **Neville Coleman Underwater Geographic Photo Agency:** 20cr, 44bl, 61cr. **Ben Cropp (Australia):** 50b. **C M Dixon:** 47cr. **Dorling Kindersley:** Colin Keates 25tr, 32br; Kim Taylor 21tl; Jerry Young, 9cr, 42cr. **Richard Ellis (USA):** 17r. **Eric Le Feuvre**

(USA): 20br. **Eric & David Hoskings:** 56cl. **Frank Lane Picture Agency:** 30br. **Perry Gilbert (USA):** 51tr, 51trb. **Peter Goadby (Australia):** 28t. **Greenpeace:** 58tr; 59br. T Britt Griswold: 44b. **Tom Haight (USA):** 45t. **Sonia Halliday & Laura Lushington:** 50tl. **Robert Harding Picture Library:** 18tr. **Edward S Hodgson (USA):** 60lb, 61lb. **The Hulton Picture Company:** 34tl, 42cl. **Hunterian Museum, The University of Glasgow:** 13c. **The Image Bank /** Guido Alberto Rossi: 30t. **Intervideo Television Clip Entertainment Group Ltd:** 6t. F Jack Jackson: 49cr, 49br. **Grant Johnson:** 54clb. C Scott Johnson (USA):** 50cb. **Stephane Korb (France):** 58cr; 58b. **William MacQuitty International Collection:** 45bc. **Mary Evans Picture Library:** 10t, 36t, 38t, 40t, 48tl, 52tl, 55br, 60tl. **National Museum of Natural History, Smithsonian Institution** (Washington, DC): Photo Chip Clark 13r. **NHPA:** Joe B Blossom 23cr; ANT/Kelvin Aitken 48cr. **National Marine Fisheries Service:** H Wes Pratt 54ct, 59tl; Greg Skomal 54bl; Charles Stillwell 23tc, 23tr. **Ocean Images:** Rosemary Chastney 28b, 29b, 29c, 54cl; Walt Clayton 15br, 49cl; Al Giddings 15cr, 45br, 48cl, 49bl, 53bl; Charles Nicklin 29br; Doc White 20cl, 20bcl. **Oceanwide Images:** Gary Bell 54cla. **Oxford Scientific Films:** Fred Bavendam 25cl, 39b; Tony Crabtree 34b, 35t; Jack Dermid 25cr; Max Gibbs 27cbr; Rudie Kuiter 431; Godfrey Merlen 43br; Peter Porks 35c; Kirn Westerskov, 49tr; Norbert Wu 45cr. **Planet Earth Pictures:** Richard Cook 59bl; Walter Deas 24bc, 39c, 48bl; Daniel W Gotsholl

30cl; Jack Johnson 51br; A Kerstitch 21cr, 21bc, 21b; Ken Lucas 20tr, 24cr, 39tr, 42bl; Krov Menhuin 25tl; D Murrel 32t; Doug Perrine, 23br, 25t, 26bcr, 54br, 55tr, 55cr; Christian Petron 42br; Brian Pitkin 24tl; Flip Schulke 30tl; Marty Snyderman 20bl, 27t, 42t, 43t, 54cr; James P Watt 32t, 32b, 33t, 33b; Marc Webber 30bl; Norbert Wu 26c, 48br. **Courtesy of Sea Life Centres (UK):** 62bl. **Shark Angling Club of Great Britain:** 58cl. **The Shark Trust:** 63tr. **Courtesy of Sydney Aquarium (Darling Harbour, Australia):** 62br. **Werner Forman Archive** / Museum of Mankind: 47cl. **Courtesy of Wilkinson Sword:** 60cl. **Rolf Williams:** 16tl, 18cr (in block of six), 59tr, 61tr.

Wallchart: Ardea: Valerie Taylor cra (hammerhead); **DK Images:** Natural History Museum, London cb (gill rakers), cb (jaw), cb (teeth); **Getty Images:** Jeffrey L. Rotman / Photonica cla (danger sign); Photographer's Choice / Georgette Douwma cb (turtle); **Photoshot / NHPA:** A.N.T. Photo Library cb (whale shark) **Marty Snyderman Productions:** clb.

All other images © Dorling Kindersley.
For further information see:
www.dkimages.com